TESTIMONIALS

Todd has captured the essence of the Kingdom Purpose behind things normally called fundraising and development. He has not only written about it, he lives it.

John C. Mulder
President, WaterStone

Todd approaches giving in a way that makes me ask the tough questions regarding my financial impact on the kingdom. Why am I here? Is God in charge of my business? What impact am I having? How am I honoring God with my business and finances? I am always refreshed and energized by our discussions and his ability to make me want to do more for Christ—spiritually, financially, and in all aspects of life.

Paul Ten Haken
President, Click Rain

It has been a pleasure to get to know Todd and his distinctive approach to the donor relationship. I feel I have gained a friend, mentor, and advocate. He has first sought to understand my needs and help me long before he has ever asked for anything from me. I have to admit that in many fundraising relationships, I hesitate to answer my phone, and many times I will let it ring. However, having been blessed personally by Todd's wisdom and mentorship, I look forward to his engagements and our time together. Todd's focus is on the personal relationship and needs of his client first. Then, after understanding my needs and interests, he invites me to join him in Kingdom work... To be blessed, and be a blessing to others.

Mike Adams
CEO and owner of Adams Thermal Systems
President of Adams Thermal Foundation

How does God prepare a man like Todd Knutson to be such a success in the development world? As a former player for me, I believe it is all about being a man of integrity, and his ability to build trust and respect by his God-given love for people. His confidence in leadership comes through living a consistently strong personal faith journey.

Bob Young, retired
Head football coach
University of Sioux Falls
NAIA Hall of Fame Inductee 2010
NAIA National Champions 1996
Winningest football coach in school history

THE
KINGDOM
FORCE

Bart & Kari,

You guys are great examples
of what I write about in
this book. I'm so blessed
by your friendship.
May His force be with you
always.
Bless you my friends!   Todd

THE KINGDOM FORCE

SHIFTING FROM TRANSACTIONAL FUNDRAISING TO TRANSFORMATIONAL GIVING

TODD KNUTSON

THRONE
PUBLISHING GROUP

Throne Publishing Group
2329 N Career Ave #215
Sioux Falls, SD 57107
ThronePG.com

TABLE OF CONTENTS

FOREWORD

Development, done biblically, is ministry. My friend Todd Knutson knows that as well as any servant of God who has ever been directed to a career in this important work. He has, in fact, given over an entire chapter of this book to explaining why this is true, and that alone is reason enough to put it in your library.

In God's economy, the work of development forces us to trust the Lord or fail. It's that simple. It calls us to life on the edge of faith; to believe in the mission of our organization, to believe in God's people, and most of all, to trust in the generosity of God himself, even when the "nos" and "not nows" threaten to discourage us.

It's not a stretch to say that most of us don't like living on that edge. We want to be safe and secure, especially with our finances. That's why I am so impressed that Todd chose to infuse this work with his own struggles and failures. In his vulnerability, he has allowed us to see how those struggles have shaped his approach to development. Actually, it's more than that. His straightforward storytelling about his own struggles is a window into how God can use us when we live in confident dependence on Him.

Yet this is far more than a book of stories. It is a direct challenge and encouragement for those whom God has called to build a ministry, or who have ever been called upon to support an important mission. You will find yourself being challenged, taught, and loved through this clearly written and encouraging work.

If you are choosing to do development for a faith-based organization, you are a daredevil for the Kingdom of God. You are choosing to trust the Lord to work through you and others to do great and mighty things. You are choosing to throw caution to the wind so you can keep your eye on the prize of empowering a called organization to build the Kingdom of God.

I believe Todd Knutson is such a man. And that is why I am so pleased to recommend this book. I wish I would have had it twenty years ago. I have struggled to learn these principles, sometimes very painfully. Without qualification, I believe that the principles of biblical development Todd unpacks in this book are absolutely God's roadmap, not only to doing development God's way, but to doing ministry God's way.

Dawson McAllister
President, Dawson McAllister Network
Hopeline Ministry

INTRODUCTION

Every year, the typical Christian tithes about 3 percent of their income. Consider, however, that if we could increase that to 10 percent, we could eradicate poverty not just here at home but throughout the entire world.

It isn't that we don't have the resources. If you were born in the United States of America, you've won the lottery. America is the most prosperous country in the history of the world. So if it isn't about the money, our shortfall must be a matter of the heart.

Note that atheists tithe almost the same amount (2–3 percent). Yet when I meet with people in church and parachurch ministries, they consider raising money to be separate from the work of ministry. These are people who are very strong in their faith walk and knowledgeable in Scripture. They're nonetheless uncomfortable when it comes to raising money, and that's because they don't truly understand or embrace biblical teachings about giving.

For many in the ministry, development means coming before the congregation and making an apologetic plea to give. I find this disheartening for two reasons: first, because they've not really delved into God's word and discovered the truth about what we're called to do with what we have, and the blessings that come from generosity; second, it says to me that the person hasn't taken the time to do their own self-reflection and understand how they view money.

The good news is that God has outlined a better way for us than this. In this book, we'll look at biblical development—what some call "fundraising"—and explore the biblical teachings that will help God work in us and through us to expand His Kingdom on earth. We'll look at how generosity can be a transformational force in the lives of both givers and recipients, and what you can do to help align yourself with God's call upon you to do His work.

PART ONE

YOU

1

BUILDING A HOUSE
TO BUILD THE KINGDOM

When I was a young man, I spent thirteen years working as a teacher and a coach. I went to graduate school and earned a master's degree in Educational Administration and Leadership with the intent of becoming a high school principal. My career path was laid out before me, my plans for the future well established.

It turned out that God had a different plan for me.

HOW MY DEVELOPMENT CAREER BEGAN

At the end of my thirteenth year in education, I felt my spirit stir. I didn't know what it meant or have any idea why it was happening, so I turned to God in prayer. I prayed for His guidance, for His direction, and He made it clear that He wanted me in ministry. Shortly thereafter, I was approached by the Fellowship of Christian Athletes

(FCA) in South Dakota, which I had volunteered with while I was teaching and coaching. They came to me and asked if I had a desire to join FCA ministry, the largest sports ministry in the world. After a great deal of prayer and discernment, I was convinced I knew where God wanted me.

I enthusiastically accepted and left behind my steady teaching paycheck as an educator to go into full-time ministry. Anyone who has worked in a parachurch ministry fully understands the faith-filled commitment that is required. You are a missionary. You must be able to go out and raise your own financial support—which is an exercise in humility, no doubt about it.

In my first week with FCA, I sent out nearly two hundred letters to friends and family explaining the call God had placed upon me. I wrote of my excitement to carry out that call, and the incredible opportunity I was going to have to share the Gospel message of Christ with kids and coaches all over the state. I made a plea that they would see value in this call and prayerfully consider supporting me financially. I fully anticipated having all my family's monetary needs met. At that time, I had a $50,000 budget that covered my salary, benefits, and travel. I prayed over the letter, mailed it, and eagerly waited for the checks to arrive.

Each day I checked the mailbox with great anticipation. A week went by. Then another. And another. After three weeks, only $2,500 had come in, barely 5 percent of my needed budget. I began to grow discouraged. I asked the Lord, *Why would You ask me to carry out Your ministry through FCA without providing the resources I so urgently need to support my family?* I was disappointed in God. I was disappointed in my family and friends. Why didn't they embrace this calling that God had placed upon me?

I did some soul searching and spent time in prayer to ask if there was a better way, a more biblical way, of doing this. One Saturday evening I came home and sat down with my wife and said, "You know, honey, I'm not sure if I discerned this properly. If this is where God wants me, why isn't He providing the resources for me to carry this out?"

My wife wisely replied, "This is exactly where God wants you. Remember, 'Christ learned obedience in the wilderness.'" I was definitely in the wilderness.

"BUILD A HOUSE"

That night, at three a.m., I was awakened by the sound of my own voice. Incredibly, I had been praying in my sleep. It was dead silent, and I was separated from the noise of the world. I prayed, "Lord, I need you. I'm lost, I'm confused, I don't know what to do. Please help me." Instantly God placed upon my heart the crazy idea of asking people in the construction industry to donate 2 × 4s, Sheetrock, carpet, and all the materials needed to build a house. Mind you, I knew nothing about building houses. I struggled as a kid with Lincoln Logs. What was I supposed to do with this? God didn't answer me. He just gave me the vision.

The next morning was Sunday. After church, my wife wanted to visit some open houses on the market in the area. I was none too excited, but being a good husband, I decided to go along. While she was touring the house with a real estate agent, I plopped down in the kitchen. There on the counter was a flyer by the contractor, and on the top it read, "'C'—Lemme Homes." Beneath that, it read that the "C" stands for Christ. As I read further, it stated that everything the owner, Dan Lemme, did with his construction company, he did to bring honor and glory to Christ.

I was immediately impressed by his boldness in sharing his faith in his marketing materials. It intrigued me, and the more I thought about it, the more I knew that finding that pamphlet the morning after my vision was no coincidence. I went to my office Monday morning and called Dan to see if he would meet me. To be honest, it took me a good hour to work up the nerve to pick up the phone, as this was so out of character for me. As my wife had pointed out, however, I was in the wilderness, with bills and a house payment and a family depending on me.

So I called him, trusting that the vision was of and from the Lord. He picked up, and I told him who I was, what I did, and who I was ministering to. I explained how impressed I was with his willingness to share his faith in his marketing materials. Then, with my heart pounding in my chest, I asked, "Would you ever have an interest in getting together and having a cup of coffee? I'd love to learn more about you."

He said he would be happy to and asked me what my schedule looked like. I replied that I was open any time and would gladly adapt to his schedule. "Well, come on over right now," he said.

I could hardly believe it was happening so quickly. I praised God right there for giving me the courage to make the call, and for this incredible introduction. I prayed the entire way over to his office that God would speak in me and through me to Dan, and that I would see him as Christ saw him. When I walked into his office and shook his hand, I sensed that he was a man of gentle spirit, a true follower of Christ. It just radiated from him.

He asked me about my faith and my ministry, and I shared my story with him. He asked me, "Is there anything I can do for you?" I was amazed, because this rarely happens when meeting with potential donors for the first time.

I took a deep breath and said, "Dan, I'm going to lay it out for you. This is the craziest thing, but I've been trying to figure out how to raise support for the ministry God's called me to, and I've not been very successful. I woke up in the middle of the night last Saturday and had a vision to build a house to raise money for the ministry. I know nothing about construction, and I can't even believe I'm saying it, it's so crazy."

I'll never forget his reaction. He didn't say a word; he just leaned back in his chair, folded his arms, and listened to me stammering. Then he said, "Todd, I believe that when a follower of Christ comes to me with a need, I not only am compelled but also have a responsibility to help." Tears welled up in my eyes, and a lump formed in my throat. God was answering my prayers.

He asked me when I wanted to start. It was August, and I suggested the spring so that it would give him time to plan and me time to share my vision with others in the construction trade.

Dan disagreed. "We need to get started next month," he said. "I'll donate a plot of land to you, and I'll give you a list of my suppliers and subcontractors. It'll be your responsibility to sit down with each of them and share the call, the plan, and the mission of your ministry and how they can be a part of it." Before I left his office, I gave him a bear hug. I prayed over him, and I praised God for Dan's desire to take an active step to do what God had placed upon his heart. The following day, I picked up our list of building materials and started making phone calls to set up appointments. One after another, businesses and contractors were moved to generosity, and I secured all of the materials necessary to get the project underway. We broke ground faster than I'd ever imagined.

I'll never forget walking into my office one cold morning in December. I noticed an envelope lying on my desk. The house had sold prior to completion, and Dan had stopped by my office following the closing to drop off the money. Inside the envelope was a check made out to the Fellowship of Christian Athletes for $238,000—almost five times the amount I'd needed, and one hundred times what I had been able to raise myself.

BLESSINGS MULTIPLIED

Witnessing the magnitude of God's provision humbled me. I was embarrassed that I hadn't trusted God from the start. That experience removed all fear and doubt regarding God's call upon me. It was affirmation that I was right where God wanted me. And it was a clear message to all of us involved in this crazy project that God is faithful when we are willing to step out in faith and act immediately when our spirit is stirred. No matter how out of the box an idea may seem, if we discern it is from God, we are called to take action. It may be difficult, or embarrassing, but when we answer the call, God shows up.

The whole process was uncomfortable for me, but I have found that God does His greatest work in us when we're willing to get out of our comfort zone. From then on, when I called someone, it was never to ask for a donation. It was to request the opportunity to sit down with them, look them in the eyes, and allow God to open their minds and soften their hearts as I shared the wonderful opportunity He had presented.

As a result of that project, we went on to build an additional home the next year, which generated $175,000. We built a third house in Minnesota. By then, the word had gotten out, and the template we developed for our projects was highly sought after and being used by other parachurch ministries throughout the country. The multiplication effect was taking place rapidly, and this model was becoming an incredible blessing for many.

In time, I reached a point where I didn't feel comfortable asking the same contractors for help year after year, so I prayed for another way. Once again, God shared a vision of constructing an office building using the same template, and leasing the office spaces out to generate a monthly revenue stream for the Fellowship of Christian Athletes' ministry. I went back to my friend Dan Lemme, and he generously donated two acres of land. Another FCA donor, when told about this vision, wrote us a check for $250,000.

This was beyond incredible—yet still, we estimated that we would need more than fifteen times that amount to complete this project.

Soon after receiving these two amazing gifts, the three of us working full time for FCA met with our board of directors. They decided not only to approve the project but also to scale it up by 50 percent. We didn't know how we were going to do it, but we knew this was of God. He would help us accomplish it—and He did. Collectively, we were able to raise donations of materials, labor, and cash to build a thirty-thousand-square-foot office building with zero debt. A $3.5 million bricks-and-mortar endowment for the FCA. This victory was for God's glory, echoing Joshua 4:24: "So that all the peoples of the earth may know that the hand of the LORD is mighty, that you may fear the LORD your God forever."

DON'T UNDERESTIMATE THE GOD OF THE UNIVERSE

In Matthew 19:26, Jesus says, "With man this is impossible, but with God all things are possible." This experience helped me see the truth and power of those words. This was a God-sized project, and I now understand that there is nothing too big for God. He is the Creator of the earth, and everything and everyone on it.

Until then, I had viewed my money and possessions as belonging to me, not to Him. Through the actions of Dan Lemme and hundreds of others involved in these projects, I came to understand that all I had came from God. I soon realized that if everything I had came from God, it also belonged to God. I had a responsibility to manage it in a way that would build His Kingdom. That is a difficult concept to accept in our culture. The constant noise and busyness of the world make it difficult to hear God's whisper. If we allow it, possessions and money will own *us*. This is why it is so important to take time each day in solitude with Him. Be still, be quiet, rest, seek silence, and commune with your Creator. He doesn't want our money; He wants our hearts.

JESUS THE INVESTOR

Once we embrace that everything we have comes from God, we are compelled to share all that we have with those in need. We are stewards—not owners—of all God has blessed us with. Sometimes I like to think of Jesus as an investor, and I ask myself if Jesus was sitting across the table from me, how would I invest His resources?

There are many ways to invest those resources that have no Kingdom impact. And if I make unwise investment choices, why would He continue to trust me with His resources? However, if I steward his resources with an eye on Christ's Kingdom and impact the lives of people and Christian organizations, then He will continue to invest with me. Being a responsible and effective broker for His assets allows my efforts to succeed.

Given my work, I often explain that I am not someone who embraces prosperity theology. I do believe, however, that when we give with the right heart and without any expectation of a return on our investment, God smiles joyfully. Even so, many Christians are insecure about our future, and we cling to our money and material things. Matthew 6:34 is very clear: "Tomorrow will be anxious for itself." Christ said there will always be the poor among us, and in my experience, this is not due to a lack of resources but because of our unwillingness to relinquish what we have. Too often, we behave out of sinful selfishness.

WHAT I HAVE LEARNED

It is important to understand that money and material things are not evil. Possessions can't be evil. Money can't be evil. Scripture teaches us that money can be at the *root* of all evil, depending upon how we treat it. If it becomes our god, it is idolatry—*the love of money.* Living in the wealthiest nation in the history of the world, we wrestle with this daily.

Ultimately, though, I think it's worth repeating: God doesn't want our money; He wants our hearts. He wants us to have open hearts, to be compassionate, to see the world as He sees it. He wants us to have a willingness and desire to share what we have with those who are in need.

A long time ago I learned a very valuable lesson: *never love anything that can't love you back.* We often fall into the trap of loving the home we live in, the car we have in the garage, the boat we have in storage, or the size of our safety net. In the end, all these things we surround ourselves with mean absolutely nothing. When we lie on our death beds, the only thing that will matter is that we are surrounded by family and close friends and that we were faithful to the Lord. We won't ask them to bring in our motorcycle, our favorite books, or our financial statement. So why live for these things? They cannot bring us peace, joy, or contentment. That comes only when you're in a right relationship with God.

In Matthew 6:19-21, Christ says, "Do not lay up for yourselves treasures on earth, where moth and rust destroy and where thieves break in and steal, but lay up for yourselves treasures in heaven, where neither moth nor rust destroys and where thieves do not break in and steal. For where your treasure is, there your heart will be also." In 6:24, He explains further, "You cannot serve both God and money."

There's not any gray area here. We are responsible for asking ourselves who we are serving with what we have. If you find yourself convicted by your answer, congratulations! God is stirring your spirit. Will you act?

2

YOUR MINDSET

When it's time to carry out God's work, the prevailing notion is that we should give from our surplus. For many, we pay our bills, buy our spouse a little something nice, go out to eat a few times, put away some for our retirement, and so on. We address the things that seem pressing but actually aren't. Eventually, after our wants and needs are taken care of, we look at what is left for God.

In Paul's letter to the Philippians, in chapter 4, verse 19, he writes: "And my God will supply every need of yours according to his riches in glory in Christ Jesus." As Christians, we are called to trust in Him for our security and our future. It is when we have a willingness and desire to give out of our principal, and not our surplus, that the true measure of our heart is revealed to us, and the measure of our faith is displayed to God. If we give only out of our surplus, are we trusting in God to take care of us?

HOW SHOULD WE VIEW MONEY?

Jesus taught that we cannot serve both God and money. This can be so difficult for us to embrace in our culture. At some stage in our lives, and in varying degrees, we are all guilty of worshiping money. For myself, the older I get, the less dependent I am on money and the more dependent I am on God, but I didn't start there; nor did I get there overnight.

It is important for each of us to take personal inventory on why we have what we have, and what we're doing with it. The quickest way to understand the position of your heart is to go through your checkbook and see where you have spent your money. Take the time to do that—maybe even right now. Look through your finances and you'll come to a greater understanding of how you are investing His resources—in His Kingdom, indicating that you truly honor Him, or in yours.

It may be time to hit the reset button. Is the money you earn meant to increase your standard of living, or to increase your standard of giving? The Bible tells us that the answer is obvious. Nowhere in Scripture does God say, "Wait, stop. You're giving too much." God never frowns on generosity.

He is the Ultimate Giver. He gave His one and only Son, who willingly sacrificed Himself on the cross for us. This must be a daily reminder that if He was willing to give so much, we must live our lives in a way that honors and glorifies Him by relinquishing the things He has blessed us with. Only then will we achieve the true peace and contentment that surpasses understanding. The way we view material things is a reflection of our hearts. The first step is to look yourself in the mirror and assess, "Am I asking people to do something that I'm not willing to do myself?"

HEAVEN DOESN'T NEED YOUR MONEY

Heaven doesn't need our money; it wants our hearts. Money is just a tool—either to carry out His work on earth or to indulge our own selfish desires. Again, money and material things are not evil in and of themselves. It is when they become idols, and they drive a wedge into our relationship with God, that they become so. After all, they can never give us joy, peace, and contentment—at least not in the long term.

I have met hundreds of affluent people whose wealth has not brought them happiness. In fact, in many situations, it brings them nothing but worry and despair. On the other side of the coin, I have also met people in the most impoverished situations imaginable. These people had next to nothing by worldly standards, yet many had such joy, peace, and hope in their hearts because what they had was in God. As Jesus said in Matthew 5:3, "Blessed are the poor in spirit, for theirs is the kingdom of heaven." Less is more. Deep down, each of us yearns for simplicity and for honoring and serving God.

To be clear, I am not advocating that we should all give away everything we have. However, I don't think God would frown on it either, if it was done with the right heart. Remember, our Creator is a God of generosity. He gave us all we have. Still, we must have a realistic expectation. Our sinful nature will always get in the way of allowing us to reach our full potential to give.

Over the past sixty years, Americans have accepted a materialistic mindset. We have accepted a narrative that there can never be enough. We have to keep up with the Joneses, we have to have a 401k or 403b, we have to live as well in retirement as we did when working. This is in total contradiction to Scripture.

In response to this, I am often met with statements like: "If I give it away now, then I have nothing more to give tomorrow. How can I be a good steward of what I'm blessed with if I give it all away?" Yet you must ask yourself, *What if I was to die tomorrow?* Suppose you sat down across the table from Jesus—and you were absolutely certain it was Him—and He asked you to give it all away today. As a believer, you would not hesitate; so why do we hesitate when He calls on us through Scripture?

Too many of us as Christians either have been poorly informed or have not taken individual responsibility to learn God's teaching about money through His word and prayer. We have allowed ourselves to be entangled in the concerns of the world and blinded ourselves to the concerns of His Kingdom. So often, we are unwilling to take that individual inventory and scrutinize our own hearts. Too many leaders and people in the pews fail to understand the need for their own education regarding God's teaching on money and His promises of blessings. We have become content doing good works only through our surplus, and do not even consider giving from our principal.

PEOPLE GIVE TO PEOPLE

In my years in development, I came to a clear understanding that the organizations I represented were only a small portion of many worthy groups. Small or large, Christian or secular, short or long term, there are so many who need so much. When it came time to sit down with a potential donor, I had to recognize that I was one of many voices asking for their support, and not necessarily any more deserving.

What resonates with people is building stable relationships. After all, if it was only a matter of the causes themselves, we would write donors an e-mail and they would simply send checks. In practice, however, donors will give to the person who is developing a relationship first and asking second.

The most successful people in development are those who are authentically themselves. They are comfortable in their own skin and in their faith walk. They lead with integrity and speak from a place of trustworthiness, because they are emulating Christ in all that they say and all that they do. This is the kind of gravity that major donors look for. We are not salespeople, but Christians carrying out God's work. If we aren't, we are hypocrites. God will not bless our efforts if they are made in a false spirit.

DEEPER THAN 10 PERCENT

It is a common assumption that the appropriate tithe is 10 percent. In Leviticus, God's people were called to give 10 percent of their first fruits, the first harvest. For us, this is usually taken to mean 10 percent of our paycheck—not after we pay our bills and take care of savings, but right off the top. If you dig deeper into the Old Testament, though, you also find that they were called to give gifts of offering above the tithe, which totaled to around 23 percent of everything God had blessed them with.

In its approach to giving, the Old Testament is something of a checklist. The New Testament, however, focuses not so much on the amount of your offering but rather on the spirit in which it is offered. It tells us how God promises to bless us when we give with the right heart. If God is the all-time greatest Gift Giver, and God created us in His image, it is in our very DNA to want to give. But how do we unlock our giving potential?

The only way is to take the action that forces us to step out of our security-first mindset. God promises us that if we do, He will show up in incredible ways. If the Old Testament model of faithful giving set the bar at 23 percent, and God promised to bless them in kind, why stop there? To go back to the scenario of managing Christ's money, why wouldn't we give 40 percent? Or 50, or 75, or 90 percent? The return on investment is going to be incredible, either here or in the life to come.

The startling reality is that none of us are getting out of this world alive. When I get to heaven, maybe God will thank me for what I did for Him on this planet with my talents and resources. (Wouldn't that be awesome?) But I would dread the conversation if it veered in the opposite direction. What if instead, He asked, "Why didn't you do *more* with what I blessed you with, when there is so much need in the world?"

I would rather die broke than face that question. None of us are taking any of our money or things with us. Why not steward them properly now and offer them to Him? If we can honestly say we believe the Bible is God's inspired word, then we cannot neglect embracing what God teaches us about our resources. How can we turn our back on that?

YOUR MINDSET TOWARD PEOPLE

Many in my line of work see people as dollar signs, and they become a means of funding their ministry that also happen to have arms and legs. Scripture, however, teaches otherwise. In 1 Corinthians 14:1, Paul wrote, "Make love your aim..." (RSV). As those in biblical development, we have to look at potential donors as Christ would look at them, with love and compassion, with mercy, and with interest. We are called upon first to look at them and determine how we can help them, not how they can help us.

Our ministry is important, yes, but we must remember that every donor is a person, the same as us, and that they are more than the gift they are giving or the resources they possess. The proper mindset for a person in development is that we are called to serve those we sit down with, not to be served by them. We have to ask ourselves what we can give them, how we can pour into them, and how we can share the love of Christ with them.

Development and ministry go hand in hand. They aren't separate activities; we're not doing ministry *and* fundraising. Done biblically, development *is* ministry. We must ask ourselves what needs exist within this person with whom we're talking. We have to have a willingness and desire to find out how they're doing and what's going on in their life. Is there something we can pray for with them? Ask authentically and with a great interest to see that person grow in their faith walk.

It won't happen overnight. Proper development requires taking time to cultivate relationships to the point where the people you're sitting down with become friends. Too often in churches and parachurch ministries, we neglect the needs of individuals because we're hyperfocused on our own budgets. Instead, we should ask our donors to participate with us, to lock arms with us in unity as fellow believers. Invite them to carry out the mission that Christ has called each of us to, and make them an active participant in it.

In time, they will be calling you to check in on how things are going and if you have any needs they can help with or be a part of. This is the ultimate goal, to help them not only understand the requirement that we be selfless with what we have but also understand the incredible joy that follows giving with the right heart. Doing so pleases God, and He wants to bless us in return. In that way, our parishioners and donors will begin to experience the pure joy of giving.

MORE THAN A SALE

When I accepted the role of president at a secular nonprofit organization, I was given the opportunity to meet with one of the leading philanthropists in the world, and I was delighted. This was a man I had prayed for years for a chance to meet while working at the Fellowship of Christian Athletes, and now it was finally time. I walked into his office and shook his hand, and we engaged in less than a minute of small talk before he pulled out a legal pad and asked me to name my organization's top ten needs.

"That's not why I'm here," I said. He repeated his request, and I repeated my answer, adding, "All I've wanted to do for ten years is meet with you because I so respect what you've done with what you've been blessed with." He thanked me and then asked a third time what my organization's needs were.

"Respectfully," I replied, "I'm not going there with you today. I really just want to know you, and I want you to know me." This answer seemed foreign to him. He had become accustomed to the development dog and pony show. The mission statement, the proposal, the ask. We must remember that our donors are likely being approached numerous times per month with requests. Over time they begin to feel like a slice of bread tossed to the pigeons, continually picked at, piece by piece. And what are the pigeons most interested in? The bread? Or the person supplying it?

Over time, we met more frequently and began to know each other better. He saw that I was authentic and trustworthy through my actions, and it wasn't until sometime later that he came to the realization that I saw him for who he was, and not for what he had. A year later I put a large financial need in front of him. He gladly responded. Why? Because he trusted me. He understood that I would never ask him for more than my organization needed and that his generous gift would be stewarded properly. The best part is that was just the beginning of the relationship, not the end. We continue to meet to this day, and I've never asked him for another gift. However, I am confident that if a need arises, I can approach him with certainty that he will respond. I have been blessed by his friendship.

The most important part of the process is to keep ministering to our donors and helping them grow in their faith walk. Ultimately, they will embrace that we are individuals who really do care more about them than the wallet they're sitting on. This can be difficult for development specialists to remember, because many of our organizations are in great financial hardship, so we rush to make the ask immediately. It becomes nothing more than a transaction; especially in times of financial crisis.

Don't treat your meetings with prospective donors as sales pitches. I've never received a large gift in my first meeting, nor have I ever asked during one. Doing so tells donors, "I've got a great cause, you've got the money. Hand it over so I can take care of the cause and we can get on with it." This is rooted in selfishness, and selfishness is the definition sinfulness.

Salespeople often have monthly quotas. Sell x number of widgets or be replaced by someone who can. That is not the business we in biblical development are in. Our work is driven not by quotas but by relationships. People give to individuals they trust and respect, not to mission statements and claims of organizational prestige. There are a thousand others howling for attention, and your authenticity is what will separate you from the pack.

YOUR MINDSET TOWARD MINISTRY

As the old adage goes, never trust a skinny butcher. A person has to genuinely believe in what they are doing or they cannot display that authenticity to others. Whether it's a church, parachurch ministry, or secular group, you must work for an organization you deeply believe in.

You must be disciplined to not jump on the first job offer that comes your way. Be patient; God has the position that will match your giftedness and best aligns with your own beliefs. Join a cause you believe in so strongly that you are willing to give financially, beyond even your own surplus, to support it. Once that happens and you are in an organization that you believe has value, and you are carrying out the work you have been called to do, the rest is easy.

If you're not willing to support the organization you represent at that level, but you still expect the person across the table to do so, that's a double standard. It destroys your authenticity, which in turn destroys your credibility. Donors are wise, and they will immediately sniff out if you are not who you claim to be. They see a lot of people in our line of work, and they'll realize if you're nothing more than a salesperson.

29

Donors are turned off by a development person who is flashy or arrogant. Overconfidence or claiming your organization is better than others is always a strike against you. To be truly Christlike, filled with compassion and concern for that person, is the most important aspect of involving a donor with your organization.

I've often wondered what might happen if a church had a full-time development person working within the congregation. This person would be called on to totally embrace biblical principles of giving stewardship, do small groups, and meet one on one with parishioners. They would teach about not only the expectation to honor, serve, and worship God but also the incredible joy that comes with it. After all, the blessings that God promises us when we give with a pure heart are astounding.

I suspect the amount of resources coming into such a church would explode. The alternative is that too-familiar, twice-a-year service where someone stands before the congregation with a budget in hand saying, "Please give only if you feel called to give." This is not a biblical approach. It deprives our parishioners, and our donors, of the joy and blessing promised by God. It becomes nothing more than a transactional obligation.

EVERYONE HAS A SPOT ON THE ROSTER

When I was a basketball coach, during the first week of practice I would evaluate the talent level of each kid on the court. I determined what their areas of giftedness were, because it's always important to make sure you have each player in the right position. For instance, I never put a five-feet-four guard down on the block to post up. That's not his gift. If he was a talented ball handler and a shooter, I wanted him bringing the ball up the court with confidence, and taking shots when he had a good look. If I had a guy who was six feet ten but couldn't dribble, I certainly wasn't going to have him bring the ball up the court, even if he wanted to. I wanted him down low on the block posting up, looking to score, and hitting the boards. When each player understands his gifts, talents, abilities, and role on the team, good things happen.

In development, sometimes people get thrust into positions because they're good at sales. Development is not sales. Discovering your God-given talent requires self-reflection. Asking questions like: *What is my area of giftedness? Is it organizing events? Is it creating donor bases and looking through spreadsheets? Is it grant writing? Is it one-on-one relationships?* Find your strengths, because if you're out of position in development, you're going to have a hard time raising the funds needed to carry out your organization's mission. If you're not able to carry out your "call" with the right heart, or if it's awkward and uncomfortable, it's time to move on and find a better fit.

The key to success in development is actually pretty simple. It requires only that you ask some tough questions and answer honestly.

1. Do I believe that the Bible is what it claims to be, the inspired word of God?

2. Am I comfortable in my own skin, how I view money, and how I view material things?

3. Do I believe in my organization's mission and the work I'm doing?

4. Do I care more about people than what they can offer me or my organization?

5. Am I properly stewarding what God has blessed me with and not living by a double standard?

If you can answer "yes" to all those questions, you're in alignment with God's call. If you can't, however, that's a red flag. That doesn't mean it's time to abandon ship, but it does mean you need to spend some time in God's word and in prayer to determine whether you are able to change your mindset. To carry out the call to biblical development enthusiastically and without regret, we must be willing to renew our minds. We must separate ourselves from the pollution of worldly thinking, and that takes serious effort. As Paul wrote in Romans 12:2, "Do not be conformed to this world, but be transformed by the renewal of your mind, that by testing you may discern what is the will of God, what is good and acceptable and perfect."

3

YOUR DEVOTIONAL LIFE

For those of us in ministry, we are keenly aware that we never seem to spend enough time in prayer and in God's word. This is as true for pastors as it is for us in development. When we're first called into ministry, those are the most important things, and we are tuned in to them. As we continue, however, we feel pulled in a lot of different directions, and God's word takes a back seat.

PRAYER AND GOD'S WORD

We have to continue to be grounded in His word because it is our power source. His word is what fuels us and what fosters intimacy with our Maker. Scripture must guide and direct us in all that we do. If we are not continuing to bathe in His word, we suffer a disconnect and find ourselves going through the motions while walking alone on our path.

Think of it like this: just because you've spent a lot of time in the garage doesn't make you a car. It is imperative that those of us in ministry stay grounded in His word, or else we simply carry out the actions and become disconnected from our true identity. We are not the organization we represent. Rather, our identity is in Christ and our purpose is to do His work.

No matter how well-intentioned you are, there will be times when you experience a disconnect from God. That feeling—that God is not as close by as He was—is a warning signal and a reminder to plug back in to your power source. All that we are comes from Him. We must continue to partner with Him and invite Him to work in us.

In ministry, many run on empty because they're givers. Having nothing left in the tank makes it tremendously difficult to minister to others, and the only thing that will fill you back up is to dive back into His word and prayer. To have a healthy relationship with your spouse requires daily time set aside to both create and deepen intimacy. In the same way, you must embrace a genuine, intimate, and thriving relationship with your Maker.

In many ways, this is about discipline. Christ made it very clear that we are filled with the Holy Spirit, the Counselor, and we must listen to Him, share with Him, and abide with Him. This is hard when we become engrossed in the patterns of the world. But to carry out the work that we are called to, we must stay plugged in to our power source.

PRAYING TO THE GOD OF THE UNIVERSE

Before we can approach a donor with God at work in us, it's important to step back and remind ourselves who He is. After all, how can we be intimidated by a major donor when we remember who has called us? How can we be daunted when we take stock of whose strength and authority we are walking in?

1. *God is sovereign.* He is the King of Kings, Creator of the Universe, Alpha and Omega. He has no limits.

2. *God loves us.* Though we may—and do—at times disappoint Him, His love is unconditional.

3. *God is faithful.* We can believe that He will carry out the promises He has made in His word.

4. *God owns everything.* There is no shortage of resources needed to carry out the ministry God has called you to do. Knock, and the door will be opened.

5. *God desires good for His people.* He wants all of us to know Him intimately, as our Father. And just like a Father, He desires good for His children.

6. *God builds His Kingdom through us.* We are building God's Kingdom, not our own. Therefore, we cannot expand it if we refuse to allow God to reside in us.

7. *God wants everything from us.* We are called upon to emulate Christ in all that we say and in all that we do. Jesus gave it all; so must we.

8. *God is to be worshiped by the way we steward the resources He has blessed us with.* He is the Ultimate Giver, so giving anything less than 100 percent of ourselves dishonors Him.
9. *God is relational, not transactional.* The Bible is not a checklist of dos and don'ts. It is a roadmap to the Father Himself, which we can follow and use to determine where we're at in our relationship with Him.
10. *God never frowns on generosity.* He invented generosity. We cannot out-give God, but if we are to follow His example, we must give everything we can.

God made the ultimate sacrifice for us, which is incredible when you understand that He is sovereign. He didn't have to. He did it sacrificially. God doesn't need anything from us; He is completely self-sufficient. The work that we're doing is worship that we express to Him in thankfulness. God could get along without us, but we cannot get along without Him. In His love, He desires a relationship with us that is primarily developed through intentional time spent in His word and in prayer.

PRAYING FOR THE WORK AND THE PEOPLE

When the check-engine light comes on in your car, what do you do? You take it in and get it looked at, of course. If you neglect to do so, eventually the engine is going to blow.

Sadly, this is what happens to a lot of people in ministry. We are pulled in a thousand different directions and become so busy trying to meet the needs of others that we neglect our own prayer lives. It becomes easy to relax in our devotion to His word and prayer, and so we drift away. We run on empty day after day without oil in our engines, and soon enough, that engine light blinks on.

I came to the conclusion a long time ago that if I tried doing the work of biblical development without God, it was simply not possible. There were mornings when I'd wake up and not even want to get out of bed because I was so overwhelmed. I'd think, *Holy cow, I've got to go out and raise all this money, and I don't even have a product to sell. I'm not selling cases of beef jerky to convenience stores. I have to sit down with people and somehow articulate to them the mission I represent and how they can be a part of it. Then I have to ask them for money.*

This is a daunting task, but it wasn't until I came to the realization that it wasn't up to me that I was able to let go of anxiety and apprehension. Once I embraced that this was truly where God wanted me and allowed Him to work in me and through me, the pressure evaporated. It was an unbelievably freeing experience; but you have to trust Him first. You have to trust that He is going to work in the hearts and minds of the people sitting across from you. And when He does, it's not because of your brilliance; it's because of what God said through you. He is glorified and we are fulfilled.

I don't know anyone who has come to Christ because of something that someone has said. We can be *directed* that way because of what someone says, but ultimately, each of us has to make a conscious decision on whether we're going to respond to *His* call. Development is the same way. We aren't called to persuade someone to give us what they have to carry out our organization's work. Certainly, there are many things we *can* do. We can explain the mission, cast vision for how they can participate, relate how it will expand God's Kingdom, and uncover God's blessing when we give with the right heart. But ultimately our words alone won't stir their spirits—God's will.

God isn't simply interested in the donor's money because He needs it. So, our role as developers is to walk alongside of donors as a genuine desire to give matures, knowing that godly transformation is always the result *and* the goal. We are chained to money and material things in this life, but we can't break those chains until we first recognize them for what they are. Once we do, God does His transformational work in us.

PRAYING WITH THE PEOPLE

In my very first year in development, I learned the importance of praying with people. Regardless of whether I made the ask, I wanted to pray with them. And bear in mind, most people I met with were individuals of high net worth. They were surrounded by a lot of gate-keepers and didn't have many ministering to them because, frankly, most were intimidated. They were very successful by worldly standards, but spiritually, they were running on empty. They didn't want to be that way but didn't necessarily know how to ask for what they needed. They may not even have known what they were missing. They just knew there was a void.

Before I ever left them, I always asked, "Would you mind if we pray together before I leave?" To date, I have never had anyone say no. I've had plenty of them get up and shut their office door, but they've always allowed me to pray with them, and to pray for them.

There is nothing that creates greater intimacy in a relationship with donors than prayer. In my experience, it's likely their pastors aren't doing it with them, and neither are their spouses, their children, or their coworkers. Our role is an incredible opportunity to be the vehicle that God uses to transform and fill them. This is an ongoing responsibility you have to your donors, because once again, it's not about what they *have*; it is about *them*. And as they're being transformed and their intimacy with God is deepening, something incredible happens: they begin to see how God is at work through the mission you're involved in. Why? Because they experience it firsthand, not through a letter.

They begin to understand how they can partner with you, and not only for the tax benefits. They consider it because they see and feel value in it. They've experienced the worth in what you are doing and see an opportunity to invest not simply a check but also their heart.

When we pray with one another, God uses that time to soften hard hearts and stoke a fire in those that have gone cold. You help them understand not only our responsibility as fellow believers but also the blessing that awaits those of us who are willing to give with cheerful hearts. These are pinnacle moments for each of you, and those mountaintops keep us going. What is more powerful than seeing God transform someone's life right in front of you? Your devotional life is critically important because you can only lead people where you have already been—and there is only one source of life. Biblical development is about leading people to an abundant life in Christ. And by knowing Him, we become bright lights in a dark world, reflecting Christ to everyone we meet.

PART TWO

YOUR MISSION

4

WHY ARE YOU IN DEVELOPMENT?

Before I left education to join FCA, I made certain that I felt called to do so. It's pretty simple: I don't believe you can be effective in ministry work if you're not called to it. If you don't have a zeal for it, it will be difficult to authentically honor and glorify Him through it.

Sometimes, in our desire to honor and worship God, we focus too narrowly on the actions we believe God's calling us to take. However, actions are merely actions unless they are empowered by the Holy Spirit. If your actions are in partnership with the Spirit, you can genuinely carry out God's mission in precisely the way you've been called to. But this requires discernment. And where can discernment be cultivated? God's word, our truth and foundation. The Bible is our compass, always revealing true north so we can navigate the path he's called us to walk. If we neglect it, we soon become lost.

SEVEN RED FLAGS THAT YOU ARE OUT OF ALIGNMENT

Too many times I have found myself wandering through the woods, unsure of where I stepped off the trail God had blazed for me. I call this wandering being "out of alignment." Just like a car that won't drive straight because its tires are poorly aligned, we veer from one median to the other when we've neglected to consult our compass. It's likely you know the feeling. To help myself, and others, discern when this is the case, I've developed seven landmarks, or red flags, to watch out for. These warning signs are meant not to condemn but to correct. We can't go where God's called us until we realize we're walking in the wrong direction.

1. *You're dreading development.* If you wake up in the morning and dread going to work, why is that? Most likely it is because you are placing the burden on yourself. It is not your work to do. It is God's work He does through you. Your responsibility is to simply show up with faith, love, and a ministry mindset.

2. *You're nervous to ask.* In 2 Timothy 1:7, God says, "I didn't give you a spirit of timidity, but one of power, love, and self-discipline." The Scripture is very clear that we do not have to be apologetic when asking others to help us carry out God's work. That timidity comes from Satan, who loves nothing more than making us feel anxious about pursuing God's call.

3. *You're procrastinating.* If you're putting off work God has called you to do, you're prioritizing the things you want to do over the

things God wants. Ask yourself, *Why am I procrastinating and hesitating?* Is it related to your disconnect from God, or are you allowing Satan to creep in and create self-doubt on the call God has placed upon you?

4. *You're discouraged.* If you are doing God's work in an authentic and meaningful way, there is nothing more threatening to Satan. He will cast every fiery arrow he can to disrupt your work, including sickness, injury, anxiety, family disruption, and everything in between. But clothed in the full armor of God, we cannot be stopped unless we allow Satan to defeat us.

5. *You're succumbing to a scarcity mindset.* Sometimes we feel like our task is greater than the resources available to accomplish it. The budget seems too big or others' desire to help is too small. But we must remember the truth: God owns it all, and if He's ordained a mission to be accomplished, it will be done. There is always enough, and a scarcity mindset is one that has succumbed to lies.

6. *You view the work as sales.* Remember, we are not salespeople, and God is not transactional. We are God's soldiers, and we are waging a war against the evil one. We are partnering with the Holy Spirit to transform lives so that they too can march as soldiers in God's army.

7. *You view people as dollar signs.* The person sitting across from you is not a tool to be used to accomplish your goals. Your work is not to nourish others by tapping donors dry but to minister to your donors directly, inviting them into partnership in God's work.

BIBLICAL CASE STUDY: 1 CHRONICLES 29

There are many instances in Scripture where we can see how biblical development should be approached. One of the best examples is 1 Chronicles 29, regarding the construction of the temple. In verses 2 and 3, King David says, "So I have provided for the house of my God, so far as I was able, the gold for the things of gold, the silver for the things of silver, and the bronze for the things of bronze, the iron for the things of iron, and wood for the things of wood, besides great quantities of onyx and stones for setting, antimony, colored stones, all sorts of precious stones and marble. Moreover, in addition to all that I have provided for the holy house, I have a treasure of my own of gold and silver, and because of my devotion to the house of my God I give it to the house of my God..." Yes, you read that right. David committed not only Israel's national resources from the treasury but also 100 percent of his own money. He didn't simply give from his surplus; he gave from his principal.

We have to remember that David invited many family leaders, officials, officers, the tribes of Israel, and commanders in charge of the king's work as well. And verse 29:6 teaches us that all in attendance followed his example and also gave generously. They were under no compulsion to give, and were not made to feel like they had to measure up to King David's expectations either. Rather, they gave willingly out of their own hearts' desire. They were led to give because their hearts were right, and in 29:9, we see that this led to everyone's joy: "Then the people rejoiced because they had given willingly, for with a whole heart they had offered freely to the Lord. David the king also rejoiced greatly." King David didn't expect anybody else to invest in this project unless he was also invested in it. They gave willingly, followed his example, and rejoiced in their partnership.

Continuing to 29:16-17, David praises the Lord in the presence of the entire assembly. "O LORD our God, all this abundance that we have provided for building you a house for your holy name comes from your hand and is all your own. I know, my God, that you test the heart and have pleasure in uprightness. In the uprightness of my heart I have freely offered all these things, and now I have seen your people, who are present here, offering freely and joyously to you." He acknowledges that everything they had came from God, and that the incredible blessings they enjoyed came from Him as well. They were only giving back what had first come from His hand. They were simply the recipients of God's blessing of material things, and they understood that their role was now to give it back. This is an incredible story and is the essence of what we're about in development. It's also a picture of what God will continue to do through us.

BIBLICAL CASE STUDY: PROVERBS 3:28

I was filling up my vehicle with gas one day when a minivan pulled up on the other side of the pump I was using. I noticed a husband and wife, as well as two children in car seats, were in the vehicle. After a few minutes, the gentleman driving the van got out and came over to introduce himself. He said, "Excuse me. My name is John.

This is difficult for me to say, but we're about three hundred miles from home, and I don't have enough money for gas. Is there any way you could help us out?"

My first thought was of Proverbs 3:28: "Do not say to your neighbor, 'Go, and come again, tomorrow I will give it'—when you have it with you." This individual had a need and I had the resources to help him. I had just over fifty dollars in my wallet, and I gave him all of it, saying, "I'm happy to do it. God bless you. I pray that God will help you get back on the right track." I didn't really think any more of it. I had no expectation other than to follow what God had instructed me to do, and to do it with the right heart.

A week later, as I walked out of a drug store, I saw a minivan pull up next to me. A gentleman got out of the van and approached me. He said, "Excuse me, sir. My name is John. I'm not from here, and I'm trying to make my way back home. Is there any way you could spare a few dollars?"

I looked at him and said, "John, you obviously don't remember me, but I met you last week at a gas station and gave you fifty dollars so that you could get home." He turned white as a ghost, didn't say a word to me, and got right back in that van and took off.

If I had allowed it to, that could have hampered my willingness to give the next time someone came to me with a need. Instead, I embraced the biblical reality of giving. When I gave, I gave out of faithfulness to God, and this man's dishonesty did not change my heart toward God. It was about my heart toward God and not the man's actions. I believe God will bless me for that because I acted in good faith and that He will do the same for each of us.

The lesson in Proverbs 3:28 is easy to understand but often hard to put into practice. People experience or hear about situations like this and don't give because they're afraid of being taken advantage of, which I understand. We are called to do our due diligence and ensure money is well stewarded, after all. But these situations aren't about the results. They are about our hearts as givers. Only God knows whether or not the heart of the individual I gave the money to was somehow being transformed at that moment. I hope it was, but I know I was called to give regardless.

BIBLICAL CASE STUDY: LUKE 21

In Luke 21:1-4, Scripture says, "Jesus looked up and saw the rich putting their gifts into the offering box, and he saw a poor widow put in two small copper coins. And he said, 'Truly, I tell you, this poor widow has put in more than all of them. For they all contributed out of their abundance, but she out of her poverty put in all she had to live on.'"

This is a remarkable statement, as much for what is not said as for what is. This widow, even though the amount that she gave was small by worldly standards, made a heartfelt gift in giving it all. We don't know how the story ends, but I believe that God took care of her needs. And this is the standard we are called to embrace as followers of Christ. We must leave this feeling of obligation to give and walk into a greater understanding of heartfelt giving as worship—and give not only from our surplus but from our principal. That is challenging, but it puts a huge smile on God's face.

BIBLICAL CASE STUDY: MATTHEW 19:16-22

Matthew 19:16 tells us of a rich young man. He asked Jesus, "Teacher, what good deed must I do to have eternal life?" After some exchange, Jesus replies, "If you want to be perfect, go, sell your possessions, give to the poor, and you will have treasure in heaven, and then come and follow me." We then see the young man walk away, slow and sad, "because he had great wealth." In verse 23, Jesus then says to the disciples, "I tell you the truth, it is hard for a rich man to enter the kingdom of heaven."

That is an accurate reflection of our culture today. We are tied to the security of our resources rather than pursuing fulfillment in Jesus. Christ isn't suffering as a result of it. God is not suffering as a result of it. It is we who are suffering, because we are not fully experiencing the joy, and the peace, and the contentment that comes with giving it all during our journey. Christ knew the chains that bound this man. He also knows that none of us can be perfect. He wanted to be clear, though, that if you really want to honor and glorify Him, give it all away.

PROSPERITY THEOLOGY, BIBLICAL BLESSING, AND GOD'S PROMISE TO THOSE WHO GIVE

Often we'll see preachers on television late at night selling holy water, wafers, and all kinds of silly things. They claim if a believer spends x number of dollars, God is going to return that investment many times over, and that they've planted a "ministry seed" that will bloom into cash. This is prosperity theology, and it's not based on biblical teachings. It's *quid pro quo* giving, something for something.

Biblical teaching regarding giving is totally different from prosperity theology. Financial giving to ministry does not guarantee financial blessing. What God promises in His word is that when we give with the right heart, he will pour out a blessing upon us. That could be financial. It could involve health. It could involve family. Ultimately, "blessing" will mean whatever God wants it to mean—but it will always be better than anything we could have intended. Prosperity theology teaches that we'll receive financial blessing in a transaction only.

In Matthew 6:25-27, we're reminded, "Therefore I tell you, do not be anxious about your life, what you will eat or what you will drink, nor about your body, what you will put on. Is not life more than food, and the body more than clothing? Look at the birds of the air: they neither sow nor reap nor gather into barns, and yet your heavenly Father feeds them. Are you not of more value than they? And which of you by being anxious can add a single hour to his span of life?"

We do not need to worry about tomorrow. We don't need to worry about whether or not we're going to have food to eat. God promises us that regardless of our material possessions, if we have a willingness and desire to help others in need, God will take care of us. That's His promise.

Giving is an act of worship, not an obligation. It is not meant to be transactional—this for that—but rather transformational. We need to examine why we are here. Is it simply to accumulate more and more things? Or are we put here to use the resources that God has blessed us with to help our neighbor? Is it to carry out God's work to expand the Kingdom, both here and in heaven?

"You will be enriched in every way to be generous in every way, which through us will produce thanksgiving to God" (2 Corinthians 9:11).

5

WHAT IS BIBLICAL DEVELOPMENT?

Biblical development means using God's word in Scripture to transform a giver's heart and enable him or her to see the world as Christ sees it. It means understanding the biblical teachings of stewardship and God's promises to us as givers while achieving a greater understanding that everything we have not only comes from Him but also belongs to Him. The more people who understand God's true intention for using what we have, the greater impact we can have in this world for Him.

A mentor once told me that the only way to be sure you're in the right place regarding development work is to assess how you look at the position. If you are in the place God intended for you, in perfect alignment with Him, you will view it not as a job but rather as a romance. Think about that for a moment. When you're in a new relationship and it's going perfectly, you're engulfed in it. You don't have to work at it; it just comes naturally. If you're not in that place, however, it becomes work. If you're in development and it's not a romance, that's a red flag, because God's work should be an incredible joy. God's call upon each of us is to carry out different ministries to different people in different ways. Like an orchestra, hearing a single horn or a single cello can be pleasant, but hearing the entire orchestra come together in harmony is a more beautiful creation by far.

In Matthew 25:40, Christ says, "And the King will answer them, 'Truly, I say to you, as you did it to one of the least of these my brothers, you did it to me.'" We are called and compelled to reach out to those who are in need. Christ could have chosen to be a king, but instead He chose poverty. We are called to emulate Him, to carry out His mission with confidence and humility. Our identity is in Christ, not in our organization.

Very simply, biblical development is not a sales job. We are not selling a product, and there is no *quid pro quo*. It is not prideful or arrogant. No matter how great the outcome, we are instruments of God, and our successes honor Him, not ourselves. I dislike the term "fundraise" when it comes to ministry. I understand why it's used so often, but I don't find the word "fundraise" anywhere in the Bible. One could argue that you don't find "development" in the Bible anywhere either, but its implication conveys these principles in the simplest way.

BIBLICAL DEVELOPMENT: A TRUE KINGDOM FORCE

Not too long ago, I was mowing my yard. It's fairly large, so I have a riding lawnmower. As per usual when I'm mowing, I put on headphones and listen to the radio. This time, after about ten minutes, I noticed that the grass I'd been "mowing" was still pretty tall. I figured I must have the mower deck too high, so I went to readjust it. However, it was set at the usual three inches.

After a bit of puzzling over it, I realized that I'd somehow forgotten to engage the blades. I'd been mowing for ten minutes, a quarter of the backyard, without cutting a single blade of grass. This is how it is when we're not connected to God. We can be going through the motions of doing something without fully accomplishing all that God has for us to accomplish. I went through the actions and took the time, but because I was distracted, I left all that grass uncut. That's what happens to a lot of us. By all outward appearances, we may seem to be doing things right. But without our blades engaged, we're not really accomplishing the work God has set before us.

PART THREE

YOUR MINISTRY

6

TRANSFORMATIONAL VS. TRANSACTIONAL

Every year, there comes a time when the Girl Scouts make their rounds. The doorbell rings and there stands this cute little Girl Scout selling cookies. Who can resist that combination? Myself, I normally buy more than enough cookies, and I'm happy to pay more than I should for them. I sure wouldn't go to the local grocery store to buy six boxes of cookies at an inflated price. Yet when the Girl Scout shows up at my door, she's made the contact, and who's going to say no to a child?

Yet, if there is any transformation that takes place when I buy those cookies, it's only in the waistline of my jeans. There is no real relationship developed with that Girl Scout, and our encounter was a simple transaction. Too often, we in development approach our call in the same way, as a transaction. However, we are doing a disservice to both our donors and ourselves when this happens because we are missing out on such a great opportunity for life change.

TRANSACTIONAL GIVING DEFINED

Transactional giving is all about *quid pro quo*, giving something to get something. There is no relationship cultivated. This doesn't mean churches and ministries shouldn't have a piece of that in their development. They might sell raffle tickets, do a bake sale, or host a banquet. This form of development always runs its course, however. You can only do the same golf tournament for so many years, after all, and these events don't necessarily capture the hearts of the people that come into contact with them. Fundraising cheapens the work that we do in ministry.

In fact, most often, transactional gifts are for smaller amounts. Seldom will an organization raise a large amount through transactional giving. An organization might send out letters indicating that a need exists, explaining how that donor can help take care of that need. The interest in that letter is going to be much smaller than if the development person sat down across the table and discerned how to best serve them.

When the Girl Scout shows up at my door and sells me six boxes of cookies, I'm not all that inspired to write out a check for a thousand dollars, even though I'm sure the Girl Scouts could use it. For that matter, if the Girl Scouts sent out a mass mailing instead of their door-to-door approach, my willingness to order a half dozen boxes and put a check in the mail certainly isn't high.

TRANSFORMATIONAL GIVING DEFINED

Instead of sitting down with the prospective donor and looking at what we can *receive* from them, we must first look at what we can *give* them. What is their need? We must put their needs before ours. When we take this approach the donor will respond.

We are not out to make a sale, exchanging something in return for something else. We are to carry out God's call upon our lives in a way that is transformational. This transformation occurs within that donor when they experience biblical stewardship and joy in cheerful giving. It happens when they gain an understanding that what we have comes from God, and belongs to God.

This is when a true transformation can take place within your organization as well. When that transformation takes place in the hearts of major donors, they are willing to do great things for the organization you represent. As such, these efforts are not gap fillers for underwriting your operation's expense. These are for the long-term future of your organization's development. Moreover, transformational gifts are generally larger than transactional ones not only in the amount given but in the joy and fulfillment experienced by the giver. Transformational development is Spirit led.

The giving is not the end of the relationship with a donor but rather the beginning. They have now invested in the organization you are representing, and therefore in you as a person. Just as with that smiling little Girl Scout, people give to people before they give to organizations. I make it a point to stay in touch with my organization's donors on a regular basis, through phone calls or handwritten notes of encouragement. When possible, I try to spend time with them, even for just a cup of coffee or lunch. If they have a child or grandchild who has a sporting event, I may go to it. I'm going to become an actively involved participant in their life, because if I'm not willing to do that, that brings into question where my interests really lie. Am I interested in their heart, spiritual growth, and welfare or only in what they can give?

Donors pick up on that. They notice the difference when someone takes the time to pen a handwritten note versus a computer-generated letter. Very few people in development are doing handwritten notes because it takes time, but that is precisely what makes them meaningful; especially in this day and age of e-mails and texting. Those are cheap, easy ways to communicate, and they don't cultivate the same intimacy in a relationship. Our God is a personal God, so if we have God's DNA, we also want to invest in a personal relationship with others. That is the heart of transformational giving.

WHERE MINISTRY HAPPENS

A couple of years ago I was representing an organization that was supporting an orphanage in Kenya. The orphanage had great financial need, lacking resources to feed, properly clothe, and provide shelter for these kids. At the time, our organization did not have the funds available to help them the way we wanted to. We talked about it at a board meeting and brainstormed for anything we could do but came up short; we just didn't have the resources. We all agreed to go home and pray about it, to see what God would reveal to us.

I left that meeting feeling sad that we didn't have the means to help out. I prayed, "Lord, I don't know how we can do this, but I know You have a plan. Reveal it to me, reveal it to one of the board members."

The next day I received a call from one of the members. He said, "All the way home, God was working in my heart. I feel really compelled to take care of this need. This is going to be a big gift for me, and it's going to stretch me. But I know this is what God wants me to do, and I'm going to act on it." He committed that day to gift a quarter of a million dollars. This was a 100-percent-Spirit-led response by this board member. He acted upon it because he believed what God has told us—that all we have belongs to, and comes from, Him.

Transformation takes place in our lives only when we respond to God's call. After all, transform means to change from one thing into something else. So as God works new life within us, we respond in new and incredible ways. There's nothing I can say or do that can transform somebody else. Instead, it is the willingness on my part to look at them as Christ looks at them, to understand their needs. That is when God uses me—and you too—as agents of true transformation in their lives. It's that beautiful place where their desire to grow and know the truth and my willingness to share it with them meet.

That board member's gift was transformational to the orphanage and to those kids who lived there. It was transformational in his life too, because he went beyond his comfort level and acted. And even more, it was transformational for all of the other board members to witness how firm his conviction was regarding what God had placed in his heart. When God transforms us, He transforms others. This is the Kingdom force—the spirit of biblical giving.

7

WHY DEVELOPMENT IS MINISTRY

When we as followers of Christ are unified in our numbers, it is amazing how God will work through us. In Acts 2:42-45, we read that the early Church "devoted themselves to the apostles' teaching and the fellowship, to the breaking of bread and the prayers. And awe came upon every soul, and many wonders and signs were being done through the apostles. And all who believed were together and had all things in common. And they were selling their possessions and belongings and distributing the proceeds to all, as any had need."

This is an example of true fellowship. The believers acted together to carry out what God had placed on their hearts, and even sold their own possessions. It doesn't say that they gave to *some* people who had need. It says they gave to *any* that had need. They weren't selective. It wasn't an arbitrary checklist to determine where they were going to direct their resources. They gave to everyone who had a need. That sounds like Christ.

John 15:5 reads, "I am the vine; you are the branches. Whoever abides in me and I in him, he it is that bears much fruit, for apart from me you can do nothing." This shows us once again how God is our source of life, and we use that power to carry out His will. We can do it independently, but as we see in the passage from Acts 2, when we come together, God multiplies the impact of our service.

It's also important to note that they devoted themselves to the apostles' teaching. They didn't just *listen* to it; they *devoted* themselves to it. They carried it out with discipline. They wanted to honor God through their devotion. They had a true understanding that the apostles wouldn't be able to carry out their ministry without fellow believers providing the resources for them to do it.

DEVELOPMENT AS COMMUNITY FORMATION

Each of us in ministry needs to realize that if God has called us to it, He will provide the resources for us to carry it out. That doesn't mean we can simply sit at our desks and wait for checks to arrive in the mail. We have to take action and go out and serve real people with real needs—only then will true transformation take place.

What would our world look like if every follower of Christ gave something? It would transform the entire world. Everybody has a role to play. Not all roles look exactly the same, as Scripture makes clear, but the expectation is that each of us do *something*.

Let's revisit the basketball team. All five kids on the court need to understand their respective roles, have a willingness to run the designed plays, and have the humility to play without concern about who gets the credit. They must be willing to give 100 percent with every opportunity they have to be on the court.

As followers of Christ, we must embrace that same model. We need a hunger to come to a true understanding of what our call is. If we do this in a way that's glorifying to God, without desire for accolades or anything else in return, God will bless us. Regardless of the outcome, I can assure you it will be transformational.

THE PARABLE OF THE TALENTS REVISITED

In Matthew 25, Jesus tells the parable of a master who left on a journey. In his absence, he gave three of his servants money. To one he gave five talents; to the second, two talents; and to the third servant, one talent. When he returned, the first servant showed that he had doubled the gift, and the second servant had done the same. The third, however, had buried his talent in the ground. The master was angry with the third servant, and took back the talent, giving it to the servant with ten. "For to everyone who has will more be given, and he will have an abundance. But from the one who has not, even what he has will be taken away" (Matthew 25:29).

There is a sobering lesson here about not hoarding what we are blessed with. What good does that do to extend God's kingdom? As God's managers, we are called to use those resources to expand His Kingdom. We are to give willingly with a good heart all that we have available to us. We are called to put his resources to work, and if we are diligent about that, God promises that he will continue to bless us.

We are not called to cling to money for our own personal gain and future contentment. After all, the servant who buried his money was cast into outer darkness. Whether it was because he was afraid of losing it, or of disappointing his master, he did nothing to honor that gift. So are we to honor God's gifts to us. Our time, our talents, our treasures—they all belong to God, and we should not hoard them but use them for the mission He's entrusted to us.

THE DONOR'S BURDEN

Donors often feel a great burden for what they've been blessed with. Sometimes they're frozen in fear, wanting to make sure they're stewarding God's money properly. That fear can prevent them from releasing that money, and make them very conservative in their thinking.

I once worked with a donor whose husband had passed away and left her a very large sum of money. The family had lived a conservative, middle-class lifestyle for their entire lives, and only upon his death did the widow have the first inkling that they had this much money. She felt blessed, but she also felt an incredible responsibility. She was paralyzed because she didn't want to mishandle it, having never had an opportunity to make any gifts of this magnitude.

I spent well over a year with her, praying with her, probing to try to help her identify what she was passionate about. My intention was to get her to a point where she understood that the money she had was not a burden but a wonderful blessing. A responsibility, sure, but a wonderful opportunity. Once we identified what she was passionate about, she was able to release the money in a way that gave her great joy, peace, and contentment.

This is how we are to treat donors. When we are patient with them, when we truly take an active role in aiding them in determining their passions, we become transformational forces in their lives. And through their giving, they become transformational in the lives of many others as well. Just as in the early Church, God multiplies our work.

It may not even be our organization that they give to, and that's fine. Our job in ministry is to expand God's Kingdom, and as people in development we must align that donor with the right fit for them. If each of us can perceive it that way, without selfishness, God will bless that. He will bless that giver, the recipient of that gift, and He will bless you as the person who helped that donor discover their passion. It's never about you. It's about the person and God's glory. When we keep that truth in first place, the Kingdom force of biblical development is unleashed.

CONCLUSION:
BE COACHABLE

I spent thirteen years as a football coach, as well as basketball coach for both boys and girls. The coach's role is to be able to evaluate each player's skill set, their mental capacity for the game, their discipline, and their toughness. Once that's done, the coach puts them in the position that best fits their abilities. The next step is to pull out of that individual what they're not capable of releasing on their own.

I never talked about wins and losses; that's transactional thinking. It was always about working to your maximum ability and leaving everything you have on the court and on the field—and if you do that, it's fantastic. But that's what coaches are for, because no one can reach their full potential on their own.

Nothing is more satisfying than taking an athlete to a level they never thought possible. However, that happens only when the individual is willing to be coached and pushed. There's no greater disappointment than working with someone with extraordinary ability but who isn't coachable. You can see what they are and yet not be able to help them release 100 percent of their ability.

Serving in development is much the same way. My role is to help that donor reach a level they didn't think they could reach. I do my homework, find out what their ability to give is, and find a way to help them maximize it. This requires, first and foremost, that I cultivate a relationship with them and gain their trust. They have to know that what I am asking them to do is out of love for them, without any hidden agenda or promise of a return on their investment.

Our model for the greatest coach of all time is Christ. He left a template that each of us can tap into to fully understand our potential. We can choose to be coachable and push ourselves to greater heights, or we can settle for what's comfortable. The choice is up to us.

In biblical development, there will be trials, sharp curves, and steep hills. You will experience the joy of summiting mountaintops and the difficulty of winding through the valleys. Yet we enter it knowing that we're each called by God to do what lies ahead. We set out to transform lives and win hearts. When we do this, we transform organizations through which other lives will be transformed as well.

My prayer with this book is for those of you who read it to make yourselves coachable. Allow God to work in you, work through you, and stir your spirit. Remember God's words through James every single day: "Count it all joy, my brothers, when you meet trials of various kinds, for you know that the testing of your faith produces steadfastness" (James 1:2-3).

ABOUT THE AUTHOR

Todd Knutson's expertise in major donor development, fundraising, and financial management have made him a tremendous asset to every organization he has served. His wealth of experience and passion for biblical development set him apart as a transformational minister rather than a transactional fundraiser.

As president of Kingdom Capital Fund, a 501(c)(3) nonprofit organization, he is dedicated to serving God and expanding His Kingdom here on earth by providing financial support to Christian organizations that embrace Biblical teaching.

In Todd's tenure as the president and CEO of the South Dakota Hall of Fame, he significantly expanded their donations base and led them to becoming debt free. Additionally, Todd served for ten years as the national vice president of development for the Fellowship of Christian Athletes, where he was responsible for all fundraising, donor development, and staff training for the United States.

Todd holds a masters of Educational Administration and Leadership from South Dakota State University, and bachelor of arts in secondary education from the University of Sioux Falls.

He lives with his wife and daughter in Sioux Falls, SD.

Contact Todd

Email: tknutson@midconetwork.com
Phone: (605) 201-5809